SCIENCE FOR THE FUTURE

COLONIZING MARS

by Clara MacCarald

FOCUS
READERS

VOYAGER

www.focusreaders.com

Focus Readers is distributed by North Star Editions:
sales@northstareditions.com | 888-417-0195

Produced for Focus Readers by Red Line Editorial.

Content Consultant: James A. Flaten, Associate Director of the Minnesota Space Grant Consortium and Contract Associate Professor, University of Minnesota

Photographs ©: Gorodenkoff/Shutterstock Images, cover, 1; Sian Proctor/University of Hawai'i at Manoa, 4–5; HI-SEAS V crew/University of Hawai'i News/University of Hawai'i, 6; Babak Tafreshi/National Geographic Image Collection/Getty Images, 8–9; AuntSpray/Shutterstock Images, 11; Neil A. Armstrong/JSC/NASA, 13; Jonathon Gruenke/Kalamazoo Gazette/AP Images, 14–15; Red Line Editorial, 17, 45; JPL-Caltech/JPL/NASA, 19; ARC/NASA, 21; JSC/NASA, 22–23, 33; 3Dsculptor/Shutterstock Images, 24; Ingo Wagner/picture-alliance/dpa/AP Images, 27; Bill White/KSC/NASA, 29; NASA/Marshall Space Flight Center/AP Images, 30–31; DOE/Fermi LAT Collaboration, CXC/SAO/JPL-Caltech/Steward/O. Krause et al., and NRAO/AUI/NASA, 34; Sam McNeil/AP Images, 36–37, 39; Jurik Peter/Shutterstock Images, 40; Vadim Sadovski/Shutterstock Images, 42–43

Library of Congress Cataloging-in-Publication Data
Names: MaCcarald, Clara, 1979- author.
Title: Colonizing Mars / by Clara MaCcarald.
Description: Lake Elmo, MN : Focus Readers, [2020] | Series: Science for the
  future | Audience: Grades 7 to 8. | Includes bibliographical references
  and index.
Identifiers: LCCN 2019008554 (print) | LCCN 2019009389 (ebook) | ISBN
  9781644930021 (pdf) | ISBN 9781641859165 (ebook) | ISBN 9781641857789
  (hardcover) | ISBN 9781641858472 (pbk.)
Subjects: LCSH: Space colonies--Juvenile literature. | Space flight to
  Mars--Juvenile literature. | Mars (Planet)--Exploration--Juvenile
  literature.
Classification: LCC TL795.7 (ebook) | LCC TL795.7 .M31975 2020 (print) | DDC
  629.44/2--dc23
LC record available at https://lccn.loc.gov/2019008554

Printed in the United States of America
Mankato, MN
May, 2019

ABOUT THE AUTHOR

Clara MaCcarald is a freelance writer with a master's degree in biology. She lives with her family in an off-grid house nestled in the forests of central New York. When not parenting her daughter, she spends her time writing nonfiction books for kids.

TABLE OF CONTENTS

CHAPTER 1

MARS ON EARTH

In September 2017, six scientists walked out of a white dome at the base of a volcano in Hawaii. For eight months, the scientists had been living inside. They were pretending to be on Mars. The dome was only 36 feet (11 m) across. Still, it had everything people needed. The scientists cooked in the kitchen, showered in the bathroom, and ran tests in the lab. Another room held exercise equipment.

Scientists built this dome in Hawaii to imitate conditions colonists might experience on Mars.

▲ Scientists wear space suits to imitate exploring the surface of Mars.

The scientists wore space suits whenever they left the dome. They ate mostly **freeze-dried** food. Communication with the outside world had a 20-minute delay. That is how long radio signals take to travel between Mars and Earth.

Scientists hope experiments like this will help prepare for a Mars colony. By observing this team, other scientists can learn how small groups work together in confined spaces for long periods of time. This living situation can be quite stressful. Scientists hope to reduce conflict by choosing people who get along well.

Many scientists believe Mars is the best option for colonizing another object in our solar system. The planet is relatively close to Earth and the sun. The atmosphere of Mars can somewhat protect colonists from **cosmic radiation**. Also, colonists could gather power from sunlight by placing **solar arrays** on the planet's surface.

Many challenges remain, but scientists are hard at work to find solutions. People may take their first steps on Mars as early as the 2030s.

THINK ABOUT IT ◄

If you were on a mission to another planet, who would you take with you? Why?

CHAPTER 2

THE SPACE RACE

Mars has fascinated humans for centuries. Ancient people studied the path of Mars to **forecast** events on Earth. In the late 1800s, astronomers thought they saw canals on Mars. Some people guessed these grooves had been made by a civilization. Science fiction writers imagined humans visiting or living on Mars.

But to carry out such ideas, people would need a way to leave Earth and reach space.

Mars is often called the Red Planet because it looks like a large red star in the night sky.

After World War II (1939–1945), scientists turned to rockets. Various rockets had been created to help fight the war. Some could fly long distances. Inventors worked to create rockets strong enough to escape Earth's atmosphere.

In 1957, the Soviet Union stunned the world by launching *Sputnik 1*, the first human-made **satellite**. *Sputnik 1* sparked the Space Race. For nearly two decades, the Soviet Union and the United States competed to reach milestones in space travel. Scientists from both countries aimed to land a person on the moon.

The moon is much closer to Earth than Mars is. But sending a crew to the moon still presented many challenges. Humans would need protection to survive in space. They would also need to return safely to Earth. Most early satellites burned up as they reentered the atmosphere. Scientists

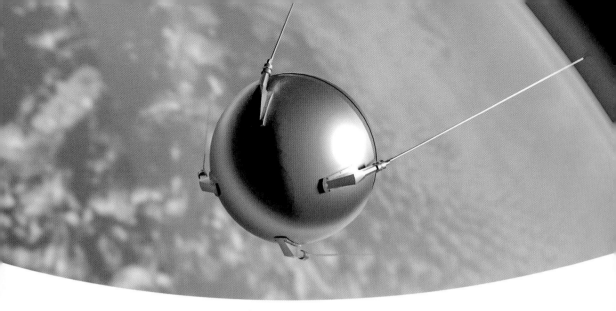

 This illustration shows *Sputnik 1*, the first human-made satellite to orbit Earth.

began developing ways to send a person safely to and from orbit. In 1961, a Soviet man named Yuri Gagarin became the first human to orbit Earth. Now scientists could focus on longer flights in space.

Meanwhile, scientists had not forgotten about Mars. They wanted to learn more about the planet's surface. In 1965, the United States flew a robotic spacecraft known as *Mariner 4* close to Mars. The spacecraft took photos of the planet.

The images showed its surface was dry and empty of life. There were no canals.

Then, in 1969, the United States landed astronauts on the moon. First, a Saturn V rocket launched the Apollo spacecraft into space. Then, firing the spacecraft's engines, the Apollo crew headed for the moon. The moon's gravity pulled them into orbit. Next, a lander separated from the spacecraft. As the lander approached the moon's surface, it began heading for a field of boulders. Neil Armstrong steered the lander to safety. Rockets slowed the lander and allowed it to set down gently.

Armstrong climbed out and took the first steps on the moon. Buzz Aldrin joined him soon after. The astronauts explored the moon's surface for more than an hour. Then they climbed back into the spacecraft and returned home.

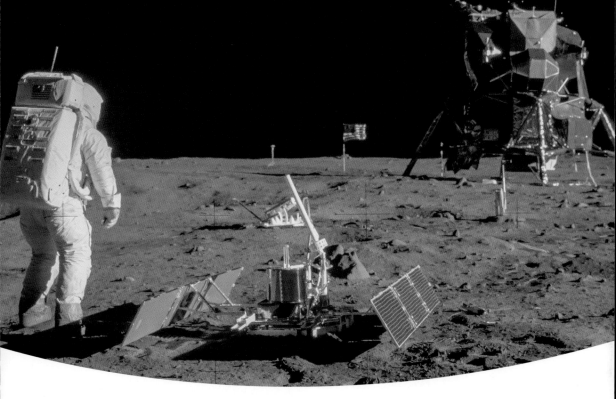

▲ Astronauts left a US flag and science experiments on the moon's surface.

Astronauts had walked on the surface of another object in the solar system. But reaching Mars would be much harder. Scientists in the Soviet Union and the United States tried to land a robot on Mars. After several failures, US scientists finally succeeded. In 1976, *Viking 1* and *Viking 2* touched down safely on the planet's surface.

CHAPTER 3

ROBOTS EXPLORE MARS

After the first landers, scientists continued sending robotic spacecraft to Mars. However, many of these missions failed. In some cases, launches went wrong. In other cases, spacecraft missed Mars and sailed past it. Some landers crashed on the Martian surface.

A spacecraft carrying humans could face similar problems. To increase the chance of success, scientists must consider everything.

This model shows what *Sojourner*, the first rover to land successfully on Mars, looked like.

Even the timing of a mission matters. Earth and Mars orbit the sun on different paths. To decrease travel time and fuel, scientists look for periods when the two planets are close together. Even then, a spacecraft can take nearly seven months to reach the Red Planet.

When a spacecraft nears Mars, it's traveling very fast. It must slow down to allow the gravity of Mars to capture it. One way to do this is by dropping into the atmosphere. Air creates **friction**, which slows the spacecraft. For some missions, the spacecraft stays in orbit around Mars. From there, it takes measurements of the planet's surface. Other missions include a landing.

The lander starts by breaking away from the spacecraft. To drop out of orbit, the lander slows down. When it reaches a height of about 80 miles (129 km) above Mars, it enters the atmosphere.

TRAVELING TO MARS ◄

Scientists must aim toward the spot where Mars will be when the spacecraft reaches it.

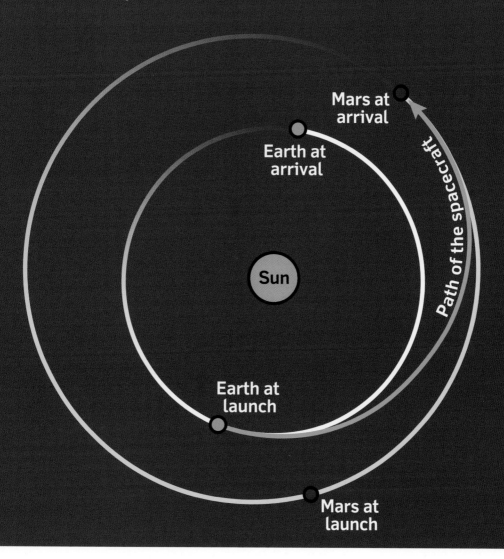

Mars at arrival

Earth at arrival

Path of the spacecraft

Sun

Earth at launch

Mars at launch

Here, air friction creates large amounts of heat. A shield keeps this heat from harming the lander. As the lander goes lower, it releases the heat shield and opens parachutes. Close to the ground, the lander fires rockets. They slow the lander by pushing upward. Some landers use air bags to bounce safely to a stop.

Other landings are slightly different. For example, *Curiosity* reached Mars in 2012. The 2,000-pound (900-kg) rover was the largest robot to land on Mars. It had to go from traveling thousands of miles per hour to a full stop in just seven minutes. Air bags wouldn't be enough. Instead, scientists invented the sky crane. As the craft neared the ground, the sky crane began using rockets to hover. The crane lowered *Curiosity* to the ground with a thick cable. Once the rover had landed, the crane cut the cable.

▲ This illustration shows how the sky crane lowered *Curiosity* to the surface of Mars.

Robots have taught scientists a lot about Mars. They have studied the planet's atmosphere, soil, and rocks. They have found ice and evidence of liquid water. Scientists now know what colonists can expect when they land. For instance, robots have identified resources a colony might use, such as gases and underground ice. People could use these things for making air, fuel, or drinking water.

CAROL STOKER

Dr. Carol Stoker is a planetary scientist at the NASA Ames Research Center in California. She is interested in looking for life on other planets. Stoker has worked with robots exploring Mars.

After studying physics and the solar system in college, Stoker joined the US space program in 1985. She helped develop robots that could search for life on other planets. *Sojourner*, the first Mars rover, landed in 1997. Stoker built a computer model of the landing site.

Part of Stoker's work involves testing technology on Earth to better understand how it might work on other planets. The tests are done in places that are cold or dry, such as deserts or Antarctica. These conditions imitate those found on Mars. Stoker led one such project in Spain. The project targeted acidic water that lies underground near a river. A robot drilled down to

Dr. Carol Stoker helps design and test robots for NASA.

look for life in that water. If life currently exists on Mars, it would likely occur in a similar situation.

Stoker also studies the data from robots on Mars. One example is *Phoenix*. This lander reached Mars in 2008. *Phoenix* found snow in the atmosphere and ice underground. It discovered some chemicals in the soil that might provide food for tiny Mars organisms, although no organisms have yet been found. Those chemicals might also provide a resource for colonists.

CHAPTER 4

LIVING IN SPACE

Many robots have reached the Red Planet. But since the last mission to the moon in 1972, humans have not left low Earth orbit. Most objects in low Earth orbit typically stay within the first 100 to 1,200 miles (160 to 2,000 km) of space above the atmosphere. Fortunately, people can still learn a lot about life in space from this distance. Many important studies have taken place on the International Space Station (ISS).

Astronaut Edward Lu floats in the International Space Station.

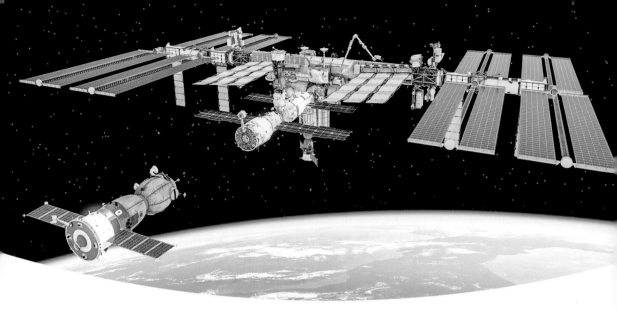

⬆ A spacecraft (left) approaches the ISS and prepares to dock.

Parts of the ISS have orbited Earth since 1998. At the size of a football field, the ISS was much too large to launch as a whole. Instead, a group of countries worked together to assemble it piece by piece in orbit. The ISS wasn't fully completed until 2011. But astronauts began arriving in 2000. Ever since then, astronauts have lived and worked aboard the station.

Spacecraft can dock with the ISS. They transport astronauts and supplies from Earth to the station and back. The ISS has cabins, bathrooms, places to exercise, and labs. Sometimes astronauts go on **space walks** to repair the outside of the station.

Astronauts on the ISS run many important experiments. They test equipment to see how it works in space. They observe living things. For instance, some astronauts have grown lettuce. They tested ways to keep plants healthy and clean in an enclosed area.

Most crew members spend six months at a time on the ISS. Scientists study how living in space affects humans. On Earth, gravity always pulls people down, even when they stand still. But in orbit, everything is in freefall as if there is no gravity. People and objects float rather than pressing against the spacecraft. Muscles weaken because they are no longer needed for support.

People's bones become weaker, too. Fluid moves upward in their bodies. This extra fluid can harm their eyes.

Scientists have found some ways to reduce these effects. Astronauts exercise at least two hours a day on the ISS. A special diet and medicine can control some of the other health problems caused by living in orbit. However, space makes medical care difficult. If astronauts on the ISS get sick, they can't just visit a hospital. Scientists had to develop technology to care for people inside the station.

For many years, space shuttles flew astronauts to the ISS. However, the shuttle program ended in 2011. Other spacecraft took over carrying people and supplies to and from the ISS. Meanwhile, the United States began developing the Space Launch System to travel farther. The system will include

▲ A model shows the shape of the Orion spacecraft.

the most powerful rocket ever made. It will launch the Orion spacecraft. This vehicle is designed to take a crew into deep space for the first time since the moon landings.

GIOIA MASSA

Dr. Gioia Massa is a scientist who studies growing food in space. After studying plant science in college, she researched a food-growing system for the ISS. Before the experiments headed into space, Massa and other scientists conducted tests at a site in the Arizona desert. There, they created a habitat that mimicked the setup astronauts might use. Massa tested different kinds of crops. Plants need specific kinds of light to grow. So she tried out different types of light bulbs.

After the food-growing system was sent to the ISS in 2014, Massa led a team that tested how well the plants were growing. Astronauts sent the first batch of crops back to Earth for testing. But for the second trial, astronauts ate some of the lettuce they had grown. Massa talked to them afterward. She found they had enjoyed gardening in space.

▲ Gioia Massa (left) conducts an experiment with a vegetable-growing system.

The next step will be growing plants on longer missions. Massa and her team are studying the challenges such crops will face. A spacecraft is a closed system. That means it doesn't take in air or nutrients from the outside. Growing crops in such a system will not be easy. Scientists must find ways to recycle air and water. But plants could also help clean the air they use and the air astronauts breathe.

CHAPTER 5

DEEP SPACE TRAVEL

To take astronauts through deep space and land them safely on Mars, scientists face many new challenges. To meet those challenges, they must create a new type of spacecraft.

One spacecraft that scientists are developing will be small enough to be launched by the Space Launch System. In some ways, life on this spacecraft will be similar to life on the ISS. The new vehicle will have cabins and storage space.

The Space Launch System will use a giant rocket to carry astronauts to the moon.

Crew members will be able to exercise and perform experiments.

In other ways, life on the new spacecraft will be very different from the ISS. While a spacecraft is traveling to Mars, people on Earth won't be able to send new supplies or crew members to it. The astronauts would be on their own if things went wrong. And as the spacecraft neared Mars, a message to Earth wouldn't get a reply for up to 45 minutes. Many things could go wrong in deep space. Equipment might break. People might get sick. Conflict between crew members could interfere with the spacecraft's mission.

On the ISS, astronauts deal with the effects of weightlessness over time. But the trip to Mars and back could take three years. Scientists are not sure how this longer spaceflight will affect people. High levels of cosmic radiation are another

▲ ISS astronaut Paolo Nespoli tests a vest that uses water to protect astronauts from radiation.

concern. In low Earth orbit, Earth's magnetic field blocks most cosmic radiation from deep space. Away from Earth, extended exposure to cosmic radiation could be deadly.

The sun gives off radiation at all times. But when the sun emits flares, it sends waves of even more damaging radiation into the solar system.

Supernovas such as this one can emit extremely strong radiation.

Other cosmic radiation comes from outside the solar system. Exploding stars can shoot tiny particles into space at great speeds. At these speeds, radiation can pass through the hull of a spacecraft. Radiation can make people very sick. Depending on how radiation hits, it could even cause brain damage or cancer.

Scientists are working on ways to protect astronauts. Some involve the design of the spacecraft. Scientists are developing new kinds of shields to block some cosmic radiation. The spacecraft may have some areas with stronger shielding than the rest of the craft. When large amounts of radiation hit, astronauts could move to the protected area.

After the spacecraft reaches Mars orbit, the astronauts will need a smaller craft in which to land. However, the landers will need to be larger than the *Curiosity* rover. Inventors are working to develop new technologies to safely bring these landers down to the surface.

THINK ABOUT IT ◄

How would life aboard the ISS be similar to life in a colony on Mars? How would it be different?

CHAPTER 6

BUILDING A COLONY

Starting a colony on Mars will require huge amounts of preparation. Fortunately, scientists can test new technologies on Earth before sending them into space. People can also practice living in Mars-like situations, such as the dome in Hawaii.

The surface of Mars is very cold. The soil is toxic to people. Colonists will need buildings and suits to protect them from this harsh environment.

Scientists test space suits and radar in the Dhofar Desert in Oman.

Computers in the buildings might control the conditions inside to make sure people are safe and comfortable. Cosmic radiation poses another threat. More of it hits the surface of Mars than reaches the surface of Earth. People might cover the colony's buildings with Martian soil to protect against this radiation.

Robots may be able to begin assembling buildings on Mars before people arrive. They might even create parts of buildings from the planet's soil and dirt. The more resources a colony can gather from Mars, the less material people will need to bring from Earth.

With Earth so far away, the colony would want to become as independent as possible. Earth would be too far away for someone to get treatment for a medical emergency, for example. Therefore, the colony would need medical

In 2018, scientists built a habitat in the Dhofar Desert to test technology that could be used on Mars.

supplies and people with medical knowledge. Scientists are also working on greenhouses that could grow crops on Mars.

The colonists would need electricity, too. They could use nuclear power, which is used by robotic rovers and landers. Inventors are also working on ways to produce fuel from gases found in the Martian atmosphere. This might allow colonists to make enough fuel to launch a spacecraft from Mars and return to Earth.

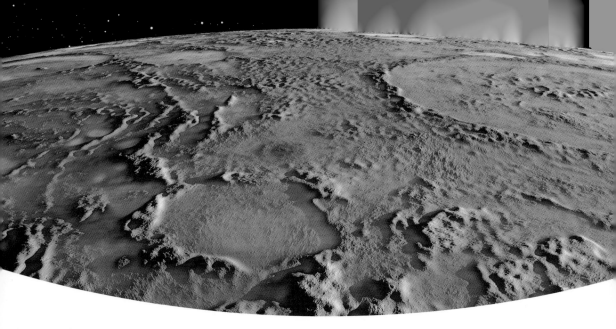

△ The barren surface and thin atmosphere of Mars would make it difficult for colonists to survive.

Some people have hoped that colonists could make a friendlier environment on Mars through **terraforming**. After studying data from previous Mars missions, scientists believe that water flowed on the planet's surface billions of years ago. The atmosphere must have been thicker at that time. Since then, Mars lost most of its atmosphere to outer space. Some scientists have wondered if people could release underground gases to make the atmosphere thicker again. This process would put more **greenhouse gases** around the planet. By trapping heat, these gases could warm the air enough that water would not immediately freeze on the surface. But in 2018, scientists concluded there was not enough of these gases in places that colonists could easily reach. Terraforming may have to wait for future technology.

THINK ABOUT IT ◁

Why would it be helpful for colonists to find a source of water on Mars? How would this be better than bringing water from Earth?

CHAPTER 7

ROADMAP TO MARS

In 2017, the United States created a plan for space exploration that could someday lead to a colony on Mars. The plan begins with missions to the moon. Spacecraft would carry astronauts out of low Earth orbit and into orbit around the moon. Over time, crews would eventually build a **spaceport**. This spaceport would orbit the moon, similar to how the ISS orbits Earth. People would live on the spaceport for long periods of time.

Scientists hope to send humans to Mars as early as the 2030s.

They could make trips down to the moon's surface and back. They could also leave the spaceport for journeys into deeper space.

Scientists are also trying to send a robot from Mars back to Earth. So far, every spacecraft that has reached Mars has made a one-way trip. Scientists want to learn what would be needed to launch a vehicle from Mars and guide it back home. Completing a return trip with a robot would help them better understand how to make the same journey while carrying a crew.

Even when humans succeed in traveling to the Red Planet, they will still need to go through many steps before creating a colony. On the first trips, astronauts might just orbit Mars and then return to Earth. Then astronauts may set up a station on one of Mars's two tiny moons. From there, they might attempt a landing.

Despite the many challenges, people are determined to reach Mars. Someday, they may succeed in creating a colony. People could live and work on the Red Planet's surface. They may even have families. Their children might grow up without ever having walked on Earth.

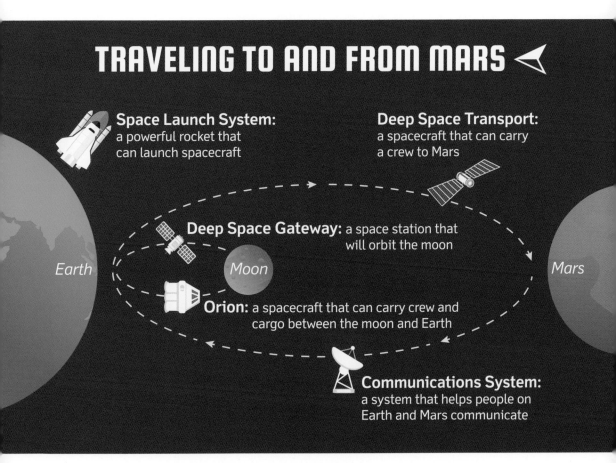

TRAVELING TO AND FROM MARS

Space Launch System: a powerful rocket that can launch spacecraft

Deep Space Transport: a spacecraft that can carry a crew to Mars

Deep Space Gateway: a space station that will orbit the moon

Earth

Moon

Mars

Orion: a spacecraft that can carry crew and cargo between the moon and Earth

Communications System: a system that helps people on Earth and Mars communicate

FOCUS ON
COLONIZING MARS

Write your answers on a separate piece of paper.

1. Write a paragraph summarizing some of the challenges a colony would face on the surface of Mars.

2. Do you think it is worth the effort to colonize Mars? Why or why not?

3. What object does the ISS orbit?

    A. Earth
    B. the moon
    C. Mars

4. What would happen if astronauts didn't exercise on their way to Mars?

    A. Their eyes would swell and make them blind.
    B. Their bones and muscles would weaken.
    C. They would develop cancer or brain damage.

Answer key on page 48.

GLOSSARY

cosmic radiation
Tiny, high-energy particles that travel through outer space but are stopped by Earth's atmosphere.

forecast
To predict what is likely to happen in the future.

freeze-dried
Preserved by a process that quickly drops an object's temperature and removes water from it.

friction
A force generated by the rubbing of one thing against another.

greenhouse gases
Gases that absorb heat and increase the temperature of a planet's atmosphere.

satellite
An object or vehicle that orbits a planet or moon, often to collect information.

solar arrays
Collections of panels that convert energy from sunlight into electricity or heat.

spaceport
A base for launching spacecraft.

space walks
When astronauts go outside a spacecraft and move around in space.

terraforming
Transforming a planet so that it resembles Earth.

TO LEARN MORE

BOOKS

Kruesi, Liz. *Space Exploration*. Minneapolis: Abdo Publishing, 2016.

McMahon, Peter. *The Space Adventurer's Guide: Your Passport to the Coolest Things to See and Do in the Universe*. Toronto: Kids Can Press, 2018.

Vogt, Gregory L. *Missions to Mars*. Lake Elmo, MN: Focus Readers, 2018.

NOTE TO EDUCATORS

Visit **www.focusreaders.com** to find lesson plans, activities, links, and other resources related to this title.

INDEX

Answer Key: 1. Answers will vary; **2.** Answers will vary; **3.** A; **4.** B